CHOSEN FROM MY MOTHER'S WOMB

A Child's Journey from Foster Care to Adoption

Evangelist Michelle Lang

ISBN 979-8-88943-349-1 (paperback)
ISBN 979-8-88943-350-7 (digital)

Christian Faith Publishing
832 Park Avenue
Meadville, PA 16335
www.christianfaithpublishing.com

Printed in the United States of America

To my siblings

You are six of the most strong and worthy people I know whose lives have been hard from the start. You showed those liars who you were deep down within. You are unapologetic in your fight for what you believe in. And you still hold fast to the truths for yourself, your children, and your grandchildren. I am so pleased to be your sister and to share in your story. I stand by your side and hope this book blesses you to keep moving forward in your journey to freedom.

Contents

Preface

THE BIBLE SAYS God chooses those whom the world considers foolish to shame those who think they are wise, and God chooses the puny and powerless to shame the high and mighty. He chooses the lowly, the laughable in the world's eyes—nobodies—so that he would shame the somebodies. He chooses what is regarded as insignificant to supersede what is regarded as prominent so that there would be no place for prideful boasting in God's presence (1 Corinthians 1:27).

Foster care was the path chosen for me. If it were up to me, I would have asked God for a wealthy, prominent life with a loving family. I was dissatisfied with my life for a long time. I went on the run, thinking I could choose a better life, and I was terribly mistaken. It just seemed like everywhere I went, my old life haunted me. It is not an easy thing to be given away by your parents as a child. Bitterness took root in my heart, and rejection seemed to follow me in my relationships. The enemy of my soul sought to wipe me out through generational curses.

My toughest battle was my own heart, which was constantly telling me I was fine, there is nothing wrong, and the world owed me something. My heart was hardened, and I couldn't see straight. The water from the Word of God began to break up the fallow ground of my heart. My heart's desire now is for the reader to peer through my testimony and begin to examine their own life in hopes that it would break through the chains of a disrupted past. John 15:13 says, "Greater love hath no man than this, that a man lay down his life for his friends." That is what I intend to do for you.

Acknowledgments

Above all, I thank my Savior, who has filled my heart with his loving-kindness. He is the author and the finisher of my faith. He has taken me from the lowest point of darkness to the holy mountain of God, and I am eternally grateful for his love.

Here are just a few handpicked from his body that he worked through to bring me to this portion of my destiny.

To Casey Family Services, God bless all of you wonderful social workers, children, and staff who have impacted my life in such an immeasurable way. We walked through the mud together and stood together.

To my beautiful foster mother, Jimmie, and her entire family who accepted me as their own and blessed my life tremendously. You helped shape me to be the woman and mother I am today.

To Abundant Life Tabernacle and the entire congregation, you all worked overtime and spent long days and nights with us children at the church. You mentored, pastored, mothered, and taught us kids with all your hearts. My prayer is to make sure your labor was not in vain.

My Parents

DOWN THROUGH THE centuries, America has been through various movements that shaped the mindset of its citizens. For example, during the Cold War, college students of San Francisco State started a protest, later named the counterculture movement. The student activists were protesting the war in Vietnam. What started out as innocent turned into what some view today as rebellion. The students wanted to send a positive message to the US government that war was unnecessary, and all we needed was love. The interesting piece to this nationwide movement was that the students opened a door to American drama. They engaged in drugs, hung out overnight, indulged in wild parties that led to wild sex, and it spread like wildfire across our nation. As teenagers, my parents were heavily influenced by the extracurricular activity of their day.

I learned that my dad was quite fond of iconic figure Jimi Hendrix, who was an influential Black musician of his time. Most likely, Jimi Hendrix brought an impressionable vibe to the young Black generation. I'm sure these youth looked up to him considering the warfarin time America was saturated in both in cross-country warfare and homeland battles. Culturally speaking, Jimi Hendrix was not only someone for the Black community to look up to but also to perceive as their own. On or around the same time frame, there was a voice being heard in the streets regarding civil rights. It was none other than Dr. Martin Luther King Jr. who was fighting for equality in the Black community. My parents were born and raised during this season. Surrounded by protest, drama, drugs, racism, and inspirational music regarding the Vietnam War and the inland war, this was all they knew in their childhood and young adult lives.

The '80s decade ushered in a darker demons' plan. In the words of my foster mother, this is the demon of drugs. Now he was already around, but he had not manifested his strategy until somewhere between the '70s and '80s. The American government called this movement the War on Drugs. I am calling it the Crack Epidemic. Some argue that the president of that time had installed this plan to pipe down on Antiwar Movement and the Civil Rights Movement. The strength of this powerful demon had established a world of its own and picked up momentum at the speed of lightning. You could look at this as if my parents were acting like normal teens, but reflecting in hindsight, with everything that was going on in the world around them, they had it rough. My parents were terribly distracted by their environment. They failed to take life seriously and spent much of their free time perusing the streets and getting high. My mother said she would see other girls openly degrading themselves. She was asked to shame herself but refused, trying to hold on to her dignity.

> You will hear of wars and rumors of wars but see to it that you are not alarmed. Such things must happen, but the end is still to come. Nation will rise against nation, and kingdom against kingdom. There will be famines and earthquakes in various places. All these are the beginning of birth pains. (Matthew 24:6–13)

> This knows also, that in the last days perilous times shall come. For men shall be lovers of their own selves, covetous, boasters, proud, blasphemers, disobedient to parents, unthankful, unholy, without natural affection, trucebreakers, false accusers, incontinent, fierce, despisers of those that are good, Traitors, heady, high-minded, lovers of pleasures more than lovers of God; Having a form of godliness but denying the power thereof: from such turn away. (2 Timothy 3:1–13)

On top of the radical society issues they faced, they also had family problems. At twenty years of age, I was obliged to make my father's acquaintance in an unofficial meeting. Upon a long-awaited greeting, he spontaneously bellowed my mother's faults, explaining away any contribution to my being fostered. He followed up with boastings about growing up in a two-parent home where his parents were married and raised their children together, using this rationale as the reason why my mother was the corrupted one. Oddly enough, my dad's immaturity did not reflect that of someone who was raised in a moralistic setting. My grandfather may have kept his marriage and family under one roof; however, something went wrong for him to be insecure. I later learned that my grandfather was an adulterer and often cheated on his wife. This would explain my dad's inability to cleave to a wife, let alone maintain his own family.

A two-parent home maybe better than a single-parent home, but if the head is sick, then the whole body can still become corrupt. I believe my dad is the product of his father's disloyalty. I remember sharing with him in that same conversation that I was getting married, and these were his words to me: "Do not talk to me about that because I don't believe in it." I was shocked seeing how he had just bragged about his own parents being married. He then said, "Problems don't start until you sign a document."

I believe my dad was seeking security in the streets because my grandfather did not give it to him. Security is not a marriage or a house; it is the authority a parent establishes over their child's life. He was right about my mom's corruption though. My mother's life was no better. Her parents were married and moved to the United States of America from Puerto Rico. Her dad was an alcoholic and abusive to his wife. Together they had ten kids, and seven of them were given up to the state. My mom, being one of them, was placed in foster care. Both of my grandmothers grew up during a time when women were handled as property rather than adorned as wives. They were to be provided for but not to be loved. It is safe to say that both of my grandmothers were mistreated and emotionally abused. My grandmother on my mother's side ended up relinquishing her rights to fight for herself and for her children.

As a child, my mother was rejected by her dad and her mom. Eventually, she landed in a foster home with values. She spent time attending Sunday school and received much-needed nurturing. When my mother turned thirteen, she was influenced by one of her biological sisters to run away. So she dropped out of school and left, fleeing into a street life. After meeting my dad, she partied with him, his friends, and his sister. She then took off to New York. She came back to Hartford, Connecticut, pregnant and heartbroken. My parents met back up soon after the arrival of my sister, and together they started a family. They stairstepped their way into five more children throughout the '80s.

My dad, who had already developed his addictions in the '70s, brought all his insecurities into the relationship. My mother was looking for the very thing she was denied as a child, which was a family and someone to love her. She thought she would build it with my dad. My dad was looking for a reason to live, but my mother was viewed more like an option rather than a family. Ignoring all the toxins in each other's lives, they pursued their own means to fulfilling a void.

> Husbands, love your wives, even as Christ also loved the church, and gave himself for it. (Ephesians 5:25)
>
> Wives, submit yourselves unto your own husbands, as unto the Lord. (Ephesians 5:22)

Farewell

ONE SUMMER NIGHT in 1989, my dad blew through the back door of our apartment, bullying my mother as usual. He proceeded to shout at and threaten my mom's friend by forcing her to the floor. I ran to the kitchen to see what was going on. My mother tried to defend herself and her friend from my dad's rage. She would use her tears to appeal to him, but my dad was out of control. My mother became his punching bag, and we became a nuisance.

The next thing I heard was an even louder bang at the front door. Someone had called the police. My dad was arrested and forced into the hallway of the apartment. One of the officers held him at gunpoint and shouted at my dad, "Don't move, or I'll shoot!" I remember yelling forcefully at the officer "Don't shoot my daddy" as I looked on in fear. Although my dad was scary, I still had a soft spot in my heart for him. My mother grabbed me and pulled me back toward her side.

Everyone was removed from the home that day. My dad went to jail. My mom went to the hospital, and we were put in the back of a squad car and escorted to the state building where they placed us in temporary custody. We had experienced nights like that all too often, and that was the final disturbance that separated our family. My mother had been forewarned before that night by a social worker to get clean and separate from the abusive relationship to keep her children.

The relationship wore my mom out! She smoked cigarettes like a chimney, became addicted to alcohol, and one time, I walked in on her in the bathroom shooting up heroine in her arm. One day right before Christmas, we watched our dad take a TV from under the tree and walk it down the street. While I didn't see my dad use, he did show us the results. For at least three years of my life, I watched fights, beatings, and out-of-control screaming and heard wailing from my mother's voice fighting for her life and cries of fright from us like clockwork. My mother came to the point where she subverted her motherly role. She would lock us in a room with our sister who was four years older than me, for her to supervise five children younger than her while our mom went out to do her thing. We would be left in a room for long periods of time. I remember going up to the door and shaking the handle, crying for her to come back.

The prerequisite for a good day was sobriety, and they were few and far between. I remember my dad's smile. It was translucent and had the power to beam through my soul causing me to forget his trespasses. My mother's kiss had the same affect. Just a touch from her would cause me to forget yesterday's regrets. Closest to normal at that time was my father's relatives. We bonded well with my dad's parents and would go to their house during the summers for some peace of mind. My dad was gentle, kind, and supportive during these occasions. He was animated, down-to-earth, talkative and had a love for music. He nicknamed all his kids and had a signature whistle for us to signal his arrival. I felt valued looking in his eyes when he lifted me in the air to swing me around.

My mother enjoyed being a mom during these times. She loved taking us for walks to the park and playing with us until we tired ourselves out. She enjoyed feeding, bathing, and tucking us in for bed. One time I saw my parents reconcile their relationship on the front porch of his parents' house. My dad got on his knees and begged my mom to give him another chance. Reluctantly, she did, but I sensed fear and doubt just from looking at the expression on her face, and I could feel it too. My grandparents played a huge role in putting back some normality in our lives from the hostile environment our parents were often exposing us to. It was like a minibreak before the madness continued. My parents went back and forth in their relationship for a while, but it always ended in drama. As a result of their inadequate parenting and selfishness, we all were made to walk through yet another portion of suffering.

After being placed in foster care, my mother fought diligently to get us back. She complied with the state's requirements and followed the rules to the best of her ability. She endured rehabilitation programs and Alcoholics Anonymous meetings. My mother would often relapse and struggle to hold on to her sobriety. During our visitations, as time went on, I could sense her distance. She was growing further away from us. Eventually, she told us her plans so that we could one day learn to live without her.

I hated those visits, and I just tolerated them because I was going back to a miserable situation. Those visits were painstakingly hopeless. My mother willingly relinquished her rights. She later shared her story of how she prayed to God before signing the final documents. Even in her ignorance, she believes that her prayer was God inspired. She stated a confession to God of how we were his kids before we became hers and that she was going to give us back to him and asked him to find us all good homes where we would learn about him. I thought that was a good prayer, but as an adult, I learned it was her way of making herself feel better about giving up her authority just as her parents did before her. Now the good Lord is willing to take in the orphaned, of course. He had our backs!

In the beginning, my dad would appear and disappear. A childhood attorney stated that I had an affinity for my father despite the accusations against him. I did not understand why my dad acted out that way because I was too young. I still wanted to believe in him, and so I held on to hope. Eventually, my dad's rights were revoked by default due to his absence. My dad grew scarce in his visits from the beginning. Out of all the abuse I watched in the home, it wasn't until I left the home that I became clear about my father's intentions. Later, I read that he did not make any attempts to appear in court after being tracked through several different avenues. The state sent certified letters to his parents' house, local news, and the newspaper. He failed to appear in court or cooperate with the state to reunite with his children.

> When my father and mother forsake me, then
> the LORD will take me up. (Psalm 27:10)

Early placements were short-lived but filled with mental damage. I watched another girl get beaten by the foster mom. I saw blood running down her face as she ran into a bathroom and shut the door to lock herself in. They had a dalmatian dog that would bite my arm. In this foster home, my dad popped up to bring me a bag of whatnots around Christmas time. He stayed for just a few moments and then turned around and left a heart-crushed five-year-old behind. The next placement was worse. In this home, I witnessed a man sexually manipulate another girl in the bedroom I was placed in. I was given a bed by the closet in her room, and one night, he came to me, and I pretended to fall out of the bed in the closet. It made a loud noise, and he ran off. He tried me again, and this time he used words to manipulate me. I was violated at five years old.

All this went on during the year my mother was trying to get us back. I was shifted back and forth from my mom's home to foster placement. I saw and experienced horrible things that go on in the minds of idle adults. It was the year 1991, and I was placed in the fifth home at six years old. It was here that the elementary school I attended retained me to the first grade because I had not learned how to read. My entire year of kindergarten was stolen from me all because of the instability I faced. I remember not understanding what being held back meant, but I do remember feeling let down. Here I lived in a two-parent home that already had another foster daughter. She was a bit older than me and very depressed. This couple was a nice couple, and they were authoritative over my life and hers. I remember being well taken care of here and going to church. The mother cooked good food, and I did enjoy it. I was given a high level of autonomy because they trusted me at six years old. I could play outside; I had a curfew and perimeter in the neighborhood. I could walk to and from school by myself. I did get spankings by the dad when warranted. The girl, on the other hand, received more spankings than me, and I felt bad for her, but she was always complaining and upset about something.

We shared the same room but two separate beds, and one evening, she tied sheets together and threw them out of the window. When I looked up, she was gone. She encouraged me to run away too, but we were to go our separate ways, and I listened. When I got outside, I took off running and had no idea where I was going. I could not believe I let her talk me into it. She was gone when I got back to the house. I can't remember how I made it back, but I did not run away again. In this home, I experienced the supernatural for the first time, and it wasn't good. I remember waking up in broad daylight looking around the room and my entire body being paralyzed. Something was sitting on me and had me by my throat. I tried to scream but could not operate my vocal cords. It lasted for a few moments or so, and I was so afraid because it gripped my mind.

I encountered two other horrible experiences for a six-year-old. A dog chased me while walking to school, but I got through the double doors before it got to me. One evening, the school hosted an overnight sleepover in the gymnasium, and gunshots were fired through the walls of the gym. We all had to keep our heads down and stay quiet because no one could see where they were coming from. Thankfully, no one was hurt that night. I stayed at this foster home for about seven months until the foster mother requested that I be moved on the account that my behavior was unmanageable.

The Challenge

In 1991, the state of Connecticut reached out to a local adoptive agency called Casey Family Services. This agency was something like an intensive care facility, and they partnered with the state to accept children who struggled the most in foster care. They specialized in finding long-term care or families who were willing to adopt. I was having a hard time letting go of my family; honestly, I wanted them back. Casey Family Services was equipped with counselors, programs, all kinds of partnerships who assisted their kids while on their journey to building a healthy, stable future. In other words, this company was a godsend in my life.

The social worker from this corporation became the first consistent adult in my life. During the summer, she decided to place me in the same home as my older sister, the same sister that took care of us when Mom would go on hiatus. She believed I needed some familiarity and hoped that our bond would help me make peace with the given situation. My big sister took an interest in me. She saw me through several hardships. Good for her because I needed all the help I could get. My sister played a huge role in my life by teaching me how to read, write, and count. I was promoted to the second grade because of her. She moralized me with all the values she had learned along her path.

My sister noticed that I enjoyed singing, so she trained my voice. She played the piano from her lessons and taught me the music scale and how to sing the correct note. She showed me how to build friendships again, watch movies, go to the library, and read books. Going to the library was my favorite thing to do with my sister. We would pick out movies to watch at home. She put some meaning back into my life and gave me a new perspective. I have always thanked her for the support she gave me as a child, her being a child too.

Our other sister and brother lived in the same town of Bloomfield, Connecticut. The four of us were in close proximity. My oldest sister kept up with all of us. She persuaded her social workers to keep her informed about our location. It was a joy for her to receive me because it was one of her dreams come true. We bonded with our brother and sister in the same town. We began to build on our relationships from these homes as the parents allowed and sacrificed time. We played, laughed, ate, and spent the night together sometimes.

The foster mother was a bilingual reverend at an Episcopal church. Here, I had my first encounter with God. I remember walking into a cathedral she preached in, in downtown Hartford, Connecticut, and feeling like I stepped into another world. I remember my heart melting after being in that church setting. I began to learn about biblical principles in this home. She promoted healthy eating habits and would give us nasty vitamins. She had a garden and would overwork us in it. By this time, I had learned and developed unprincipled behaviors from the other foster homes and the kids that were there. I stole, used foul language, fought, was outright intrusive, and had no boundaries. After being molested several times, I had also developed a heightened sexual drive.

Some kids went to school to learn, but I went to school to entertain and to be entertained. School was like an amusement park. I could let loose and be free. No one knew about the prison I was in, in my mind. I did make friends easily because of my outgoing personality. I quickly found a close friend. We had two things in common, and that was enough: we could both sing, and we were both orphaned. I became a distraction to other children, and the relationships I built were not very meaningful. I had potential, but I was misinformed, and so my relationships became toxic. I picked up on how teachers seemed to be legitimately concerned about my welfare. When I noticed this, I quite heavily leaned on them for emotional bonding.

By seven, I liken my sexual drive to that of a predator. I stole from stores things like food and candy; this I picked up from living with my biological parents, and it stayed with me in my earlier years of foster care. The reverend tried to help me in her own way with stern and abusive discipline. She would give me cold showers, leave me in a basement all day without food or the use of a restroom, give me whoopings with extension cords and tree limbs, and slap me across the face. She enforced hard labor by making me do all the chores and having me spend long hours in the garden, which had all kinds of wildlife. She was empty and without compassion. She made me feel like I was someone else's child. There were two horrible events that happened in this home. First, I was almost choked unconscious by another kid who came over for a visit. Then one day, a man drove by the house in a blue car while I was playing outside in the driveway and offered me some candy. I was walking to approach the car to get the candy, and my sister came outside to grab me back, and the guy drove off. My sister saved my life.

The social worker eventually removed me from the reverend's home on account of a letter that came from a therapist during treatment. The therapist observed how uninterested the reverend was in caring for me. She stated in this letter that the reverend referred to me as the bad child and my sister as the good child. She stated that the reverend found herself in a power struggle with me—even during one of the summer meetings, I had on a winter jacket. She said I showed up to appointments with holes in my clothes and that the reverend did not seem to take as much interest in me as she did in my sister. She said I would benefit from a home that was willing to take care of me long term and be actively involved with my counseling. Although my sister still lived there, I was thrilled to be leaving. I insisted she leave too because she wasn't getting the love of a mother either, but she stayed. I had to say goodbye to the friends I made at school, and it broke a lot of little hearts. Those kids really liked me. Some of them cried asking why. Some felt bad for me. I had built up a pain tolerance for my situation, and so I was numb.

By the summer of '93, I was eight and on my way to another foster home in East Hartford, Connecticut. This was a two-parent home, and the mother was raising two teens from a previous relationship. The parents were engaged, and they were both from Puerto Rico. My social worker thought I could benefit from being surrounded by those who could teach me more about my culture. In the beginning, I liked this home because I was the youngest in the family. Right at the start, I got a lot of attention. The mother seemed to have a positive attitude, and it appeared to be a fresh, clean start for me. As soon as I got there, the mother rearranged my appearance. She pierced my ears, cut my hair, and gave me a new wardrobe. She took an interest in giving me a confidence boost and lifted my self-esteem. I felt like a princess doll in her home. I had never noticed my beauty until this placement. I was constantly told how beautiful I was by strangers, but I never paid them any mind because I felt like a reject, so it didn't matter. I was tested for special education in this home and placed on academic disability with a diagnosis of ADHD, another label. I received accommodations while in school as if I could not learn on my own. I remember having to take lots of tests and different people coming to the school to pull me out of class and talk to me about my life. I did not have a normal childhood. I was placed in therapeutic camps with other children who were struggling to manage their issues. Things took a turn for the worse in this home because the fiancé began to take inappropriate looks at me. He proceeded to carry on a perverse relationship with me in their home, but it happened over time.

He approached me as a father figure. He was gentle, kind, and concerned, just like a dad. He used smooth words and used tricky devices like food and candy to harass me. He built a trustworthy relationship with me that took him about a full year to break through. I grew to appreciate his kindness and affection toward me. All we had were words, food, candy, playtime, and movies. At eight years old, I thought he was doing great! A year later, after turning nine, we moved out of that home and moved into an upgrade on the other side of East Hartford. I remember him opening up to me about the mother and what she wasn't doing for him. He was always a sexually active guy, touching her inappropriately in front of us. She would always shrug him off. He manipulated me for several months by confiding in me and talking to me about their issues. He made me feel like we were the outcasts in the home, and all we had was each other.

> Be sober, be vigilant, because your adversary the
> devil walketh about as a roaring lion, seeking
> whom he may devour. (1 Peter 5:8)

Aside from him sharing their personal business, it seemed like he was trying to be a father. I felt like a princess of some sort because he was always lifting me up. After moving into the new home, our harmless relationship grew to me being his girlfriend. One day, I was caught off guard by him because I was running through the house, playing and laughing, when he cornered me. He pressed himself against me frontward and told me that we were girlfriend and boyfriend. Something inside me wanted to scream, but by that time I was scared.

Things grew worse from there, and he began to harass me every day before school because we were the last two to leave the house. The discomfort in my heart made me grow resistant, and he began to threaten and verbally abuse me. One day while at the after-school program, the therapist pulled me in her office and asked if I was okay and if I needed to talk. She shared about how bubbly and energetic I was but had noticed a big shift in my personality. She began to probe in my homelife. As she spoke, I could sense my emotions coming up in my esophagus into my throat and in my mouth, but I still did not say anything. She then said the open-door words, "It's okay. You can tell me, and it will remain confidential." She gave me her word that she would not tell anyone else.

As soon as I heard those words, I trusted her and blurted out, "My foster dad is touching me." She was in shock, but she kept herself together long enough to pull out further details of the situation. She then proceeded to make a phone call. A huge investigation took place while I remained in the home. I was cornered and yelled at by him and his fiancée. They called me a liar, and the entire family ostracized me until the state found an emergency placement for me. I did get a chance to see that all the scare tactics he used against me were lies. He was not criminally charged with molestation by the state, but CFS revoked his license to foster any more children.

The social worker scheduled an appointment for me at the hospital out of protocol. I felt violated all over again. Children are coerced and fed thoughts by adults, especially when they are not being patient or compassionate. It is even worse for the child when they are already viewed as the problem. Such was the case with me. Instead of being taught, I was labeled. I was perceived as one who did anything to get attention, positive or negative. That was true, but at what point do you teach the child the correct way to go? Up until that point, the only person who taught me anything was my eleven-year-old sister.

The emergency placement was in the custody of a single Black businesswoman who lived in Bristol, Connecticut. The social worker informed me that this would be temporary until she finds a permanent home. Blah, blah, blah was eventually all I heard from the social worker. Back then, social workers were there for feel-good moments and pity trips. Literally, I could get any social worker to do just about anything for me to make me smile. They didn't care; they were doing their job and believed that if it brought some sense of relief and cooperation, then that's what was done. For example, there was a local restaurant in Connecticut by the name of Friendly's. Friendly's was a diner slash ice cream bar. To me, they were known for their five-scooper sundae that you could top with any flavor you wanted! Any social worker who wanted to make me happy had to take me to Friendly's.

So I remember the businesswoman like yesterday. She picked me up from Casey Family Services on a rainy night, and we took a long drive to Bristol, Connecticut. She listened to jazz music and female artists of old like Billie Holliday and Ella Fitzgerald, just to name a couple. She had class but no partner. She made her own money and was the boss. She believed in independence, being the head, and making a good living. She gave me the skinny and ran down the drill as soon as we got to her house. She told me her home was a temporary placement. She went further to say that it is because she doesn't do kids. Apparently, my situation was a desperate one, and she was doing me a solid.

In a way, I was alright with her honesty because I had been on autopilot since I was five years old, and I was intrigued to meet an up-front adult. I wasn't living to get attached to anyone by this time; I was living to experience pleasure if I could. I established a fantasy world in my mind. I studied her so I knew when to come out and how to speak her language. I transitioned smoothly. I begin to do better in school except now, I rode the short bus for the mentally challenged kids. I was embarrassed by this because everyone knew that the short bus was for "special children," and so that was how I was seen. I did not get bullied at this school, but I did not make many friends either. Anywhere I went, I found one person whom I could confide in and hang around. The state found me another therapeutic program with a lot of children who had problems and did not care about their lives. I hated those programs because I did not believe I should have been there. No one wanted to invest in me; they just stuck me somewhere I could be watched.

Life wasn't all that bad in Bristol, and that was because I was a very cooperative child at this point. I did not put up the fight I should have. They say I was a fighter, but I say I was passive and allowed the state to do what they were going to do regardless. So the business lady ended up spoiling me by lavishing me with her money. I spent two Christmases at her home, and each Christmas, I received expensive gifts. She turned her house into a Christmas wonderland. She bought me so much stuff that she remodeled and finished her basement on my account. One of the rooms was my toy room, and it was decked out!

She took me on my first flight, and we were off to Cape Cod, Massachusetts. She planned itineraries where we would have something to do each day and sometimes multiple sites in one day, including boat rides. The next trip was every child's dream, Walt Disney World. She had a niece around my age that she introduced me to, and she took her along as a companion. She took me on her business trips which were luxurious. If I carried myself well and stayed out of her way, she laid out the red carpet and paid me back with pleasure and gifts. It was like we had a secret contract. She purchased all kinds of pet animals for me. She herself owned two dogs that she kept up with. All my animals died because I did not really know how to take care of them, and she didn't take time to really teach me. So I would bury them in the backyard. Every now and again I would do something childish, and she would remember I was a child, but it really got under her skin. I was left alone outside before school started because she had to go to work early, and I would be left outside after school waiting on her to get home from work. I had no respect for her, so if she tried to discipline me, I would put her back in the place she said she wanted to be—that she was not my mother. One day she revealed a secret that she had a son that she had helped raise. He was in his early twenties. She told me he was constantly in trouble and was in and out of jail. He stayed with us one weekend and slept in my room. My foster cousin and I shared the bed by the window, and he took the other. He crawled in our bed and proceeded to sexually coerce us. Maybe I had gained some courage from the previous incidents where I had not spoken up because this time I did. Maybe I wanted to protect the other girl who seemed to be unhappy with the fact that he chose to try to seduce me first. Either way, I knew it was wrong, and I felt more power to stand up, so I did.

> And the Lord said, Simon, Simon, behold, Satan
> hath desired to have you, that he may sift you as
> wheat: But I have prayed for thee, that thy faith
> fail not: and when thou art converted, strengthen
> thy brethren. (Luke 22:31–32)

I was to be integrated into yet another home because I told my social worker too about the midnight escapade the businesswoman's son wanted to have with two little girls. I immediately started respite weekends with a nun from the Catholic Church. She was financially hospitable like the business lady, except the nun played with me and participated in activities with me. She would take me to local community events like Christmas plays with Charles Dickens storytelling, petting zoos, swimming at the YMCA, ice-skating at a local rink, bike riding trails, restaurants, and all kinds of natural adventures. She enjoyed my company, and she showed me by reading to me books like *Anne of Green Gables*, *Huckleberry Finn*, *Gulliver's Travels*, the Bible, and many other books. She taught me etiquette by engaging in table activities like tea and cake with me. She showed me how to be classy, do house chores properly, cook a little, and many other household activities.

While I was there at the nun's house, I would have horrible nightmares. I would tell her, and she taught me how to change my thoughts while sleeping. She said I was in control and that if I changed my thought, the nightmare would change. So the next time I had a nightmare, I changed my thought, and the nightmare shifted to a dream of whatever I wanted to think about. I thought she was a genius. I looked up to her as a religious lady because she was so kind and giving, and it seemed like there was nothing I could do to get under her skin, not that I tried. She always kept me occupied, and she remained interested in whatever I liked. If she had to go to church and do something, she trusted me to stay back at her home. She would promise to do something with me if I did well while she was out. I never let her down. I still say she was a kind woman.

The single businesswoman had type 2 diabetes. She had nurses on call that treated her illness at the house. She did not like to be exposed, and she did not want pity. She tried to be outgoing for the time that she had me, but she retreated like a hermit crab when she had enough.

Up until that point, I was exposed to several religious beliefs. I experienced Jehovah's Witnesses, Catholic, Baptist, and other denominations under Catholicism. Moving from home to home and city to city gave me diversity in many areas of my life.

The social worker brought more sad news that year. She said that my being ten put me at a disadvantage in finding placement. I was considered a troubled teen with extensive baggage that needed round-the-clock attention. She said they would have to find a group home for me if a family was not an option. That was hard news to bear. I was moving forward but having a hard time gaining perspective. I did not want to leave the business lady because I had become used to the high life and attached to all the things I received in her care. I thought I grew fond of her, but in truth, I grew to care about the same things she did. I thought we had a connection, but I was too young to realize that she had purchased my affection.

> For the love of money is the root of all evil: which while some coveted after, they have erred from the faith, and pierced themselves through with many sorrows. (1 Timothy 3:16)

Reborn

It was May 31, 1995, and I was turning eleven years old in three days. My file was extensive and enough to make any foster parent think thrice. Although I had respite time with the nun, I could not move in with her; she was strictly respite. So I began respite with an older woman named Evangelist Jimmie. This woman was a preacher and strong in her faith. She had three adult children and four grandchildren around my age when I met her. She was originally from Dawson, Georgia, but relocated to Connecticut in her youth. She had a family-owned business, a beauty salon, where she worked full-time as a professional stylist, along with her youngest daughter.

Meeting her for the first time was nothing like any of the other homes. It was awkward being in her presence, and I didn't know how to act, so I stood there and stared. She would try to make me laugh by saying, "Come here. I'm not going to bite." I never thought she was, but just her saying that made me think she would, so I kept my distance. To my surprise, she accepted the difficult task of raising Michelle. Her birthday was June 1, and my birthday was June 2. And both of our middle names were Lee. I remember the day I arrived like it happened yesterday. After hauling my luggage into my new bedroom, she stated in the presence of the social worker, "I am your mother now, and I will not treat you any different than I treated my own kids. That means that if I must discipline you, then I will, and this will be your last home." I believed every word she said because she was so sure of herself. She went on to tell me about the rules in her home and how I would be disciplined if I disobeyed.

The evangelist attended an Apostolic Pentecostal church and was Holy Spirit filled and driven. She was unique and had my attention like a rookie soldier on his first day in the field. Her home felt like the cathedral I went into when I was a little girl. For the first time, I took a deep breath and trusted. Right from the beginning, she set out to dismantle the lies of this devil she went on about. She inquired about some of the things that were written about me. She began pulling out information and replacing it with this Bible she went on about. She was embarrassed by some of the things I knew. I remember her sharing that I knew things that she did not and did not want to know, for that matter, but that she would do her best to teach me the right way.

There was nothing my mother withheld from me. She communicated with me, brought me to church, brought me to school, studied the Bible with me, counseled me, played with me, taught me how to pray, and prayed for me. She began to read the Bible to me effective immediately. We read at home, at her shop, and at church. She said it was going to save my life. A memorable moment with my mom was the evening she came into my room and kneeled at the side of my bed, beckoning me to join her. She asked me how I felt about my parents while we were down there. I told her that I missed them, and they were alright with me. She said that how I felt about them would determine the rest of my life, and forgiving them would help me.

She told me what happened to them and why they were unfit to be parents. My mother referred to drugs as demons, and neither one of them could shake them off their backs. She then said that God would save them if I prayed for them. That was the night she taught me how to ask in prayer. She prayed and cried hard tears for my parents to be set free from the "demon of drugs" and receive the salvation of the Lord. I believed and picked up the torch she was passing to me that evening. It did not take me long to call her mom, and she was pleased to hear that.

> Train up a child in the way he should go, And
> when he is old he will not depart from it.
> (Proverbs 22:6)

My mother went through a major adjustment after welcoming me into her home. She sacrificed and made the necessary changes she believed it would take to give me the family I never had. She worked late nights to make the money she needed to move us from Hartford to Bloomfield. In Hartford, I had to ride the city transit to get around. I was mature for my age, and I did well to get around, but my mother did not want me traveling like that. She was trying to give me a childhood as much as she could. Her oldest daughter became involved and took on the task of co-raising me along with her two sons. To keep a watchful eye over me, I attended the same school as her youngest son. I graduated sixth grade in elementary school, and everyone was there to see me get promoted to middle school. As a family, we would go out to eat, visit amusements parks, participate in Little League sports, go to playgrounds and barbecues. For the first time, I experienced a genuine family and support within.

My sister would give our mother some perspective about stylish fashions for me because she was up in age and didn't know of the latest trends for children. Two years in a row, we went shopping in New York to purchase our school clothes. My sister convinced her by sharing how kids at school can be mean and cruel when others are not wearing updated clothes. My mother understood because she wanted to boost my confidence and self-esteem. My older sister always looked out for my mother and me so that the relationship would work despite the gap in age between us.

Our vacations were made to mother's hometown in Dawson, Georgia, where we would visit much of her extended family including her mother. We would drive around her old community as she reminisced, giving me all the details of her upbringing. We would go to all her relatives and local neighbor's houses. We enjoyed fish fries with the community as they would all come together to eat at a neighbor's house. I remember while the other kids would play outside after eating, my mother and I would be cleaning the kitchen. I asked why we had to clean up somebody else's house, and she would say, "Shelly, don't ever give anybody nothing to say about you. You always do the right thing even if others are not."

On Sundays, no matter what went on during the week, everyone was in church and had a role. I used to love the sound of a group of children with country accent singing in the choir. Food used to be a scarce item for me but not in this home. I never missed a meal. I remember the year her mother became ill and endured amputations. My mother and I would go to Georgia to be with her and nurse her. My mother and I would bathe her and get her dressed, and I would put her to sleep by reading the Bible to her. She is the reason why I became a nurse for the elderly in my twenties.

I soaked up every bit of the attention my mom's loved ones gave me. Not everybody in my mother's family accepted me though. Some family members understood her mission, but others did not and, quite frankly, did not care. My mother protected me with wisdom from the Bible. She had no problem standing up for righteousness. I remember feeling ostracized at times by others, but nothing got past my mom. She had an eagle's eye and would take authority, and if she missed something, my older sister caught it and would encourage the best way she knew how. As if the beautiful relationship I had with the evangelist and her family was not already good enough, I received a double portion. My mother had a church family, and I spent just as much time with them, if not more.

We had a homelife and a church life. Tuesday night was for prayer, Wednesday night for Bible study, Thursday or Saturday was choir rehearsal, and Sunday, of course, was church. We prayed, fasted, shut inside the church overnight to pray, and took road trips together. At the time, our church was founded in the Bronx, New York, and the second location was in Hartford, Connecticut. I went to church with several other girls around my age. At first, the girls wondered about me, but eventually, we all discovered we were all quite the same and dealt with similar family issues. Two of us were fosters, and the other girls were being raised by a relative. So one Sunday, the girls were in prayer, and they were crying and spitting up. The service was strange and terrifying to me. I cried, and the teacher took me and sat me on her lap. While consoling me, she explained that they were praying, being set free from the presence of demonic spirits, and crying out for the Holy Ghost to fill their hearts.

I had been to various churches and multiple denominations, but I had not experienced anything that involved before. The teacher was kind, and the kids were transparent. The atmosphere eventually caused me to be open about my life and what I was going through. We had two teachers for the kid's department and many mentors. I learned all about Jesus Christ and how imperative it was for me to build a relationship with him. After hearing the Gospel explained and the unfailing love he displayed for all mankind, it broke my heart instantly, and I gave my life to Jesus Christ at eleven. That same year, I was told by the teacher that I was the jewel in my biological family. I had no idea what the spiritual weight of that word meant.

After relocating to the suburbs in Bloomfield, Connecticut, I was just in time for middle school. To my surprise, I reunited with the kids from the elementary school I went to back in '91 when I lived with my sister. I surprised my childhood best friend in the lunch line. We cried and laughed at how big and tall we were, and then we tested our vocals to see if we still had talent. I gave all the students from elementary a shock that school year. No one expected to see me again, much less discover what happened to me. It was an even greater surprise to know how big of an impression I made on my second-grade class. I was answering questions over a few months, and other kids who didn't know me wanted to know what the big deal was about Michelle. I was the class superstar, and I was more than willing to share my testimony, especially the newfound peace I had just received in church with my new families.

> Peace I leave with you, my peace I give unto you:
> not as the world giveth, give I unto you. Let not
> your heart be troubled, neither let it be afraid.
> (John 14:27)

Turning thirteen was nothing short of amazing. I was planted in a good home with a mother who loved and wanted the best for me. I belonged to an extraordinary church, with peers who knew my struggle was real and could relate to my situation. I had the admiration of my classmates as they were receptive to my testimony. Finally, I had another divine encounter with Jesus Christ. Annually, the church would go to a Christian retreat on Blue Mountain in New Ringgold, Pennsylvania. All of us kids were always so excited because it would be like a huge sleepover party. It was quite the experience. The church rented a coach bus that would drive to our other church located in the Bronx, New York. We would pick up others from there and ride down to Pennsylvania as a congregation. To me, it was a huge family reunion. Words cannot express how monumental those experiences were for me. In earlier years of my journey, I was surrounded by adults who could have cared less, and now all the adults were concerned about my welfare and that of one another. I could not get away with anything, and I did not mind. I loved every minute of the attention.

That year, our youth teacher came with us, and the entire youth department were housed in the same dorm. Talk about a child's dream fulfilled. We were all on fire for the Lord and supported one another in a special way. I had prayed the confession of salvation at the altar at eleven, but I had not been filled with the Holy Ghost yet. There had been an altar call given by Pastor Jason Alvarez who was the guest speaker and musician that day, and he said these exact words, "If you want the Holy Ghost, then get down here to the altar now." I had been seeking the Holy Ghost for two years, and I was just about to give up. My teacher looked at me and said, "Don't you want the Holy Ghost?" I nodded my head yes, and she said, "Then go up there."

I ran to the altar, and he told us to close our eyes, lift our hands, and focus on Jesus. I could hear Pastor Alvarez's voice going from left to right. I could barely feel his finger on my forehead for just a second. In that same second, I felt a strong wind. It blew me down to the floor. I fell straight back and was knocked out. When I came to, I opened my eyes and saw others lying on the floor as well. Ushers were picking us up off the floor. To my astonishment, I could hear myself talking and feel tears running down my face. As I paid attention to what I was saying, it wasn't English. I was speaking another language. As the usher lifted me up my weightless body, I regained my composure through the strength that was present with me. I was crying from such a deep place of power. In an instant, I felt lighter, clearer, and happier. I didn't know how dark a place my mind was in until that moment. My communication changed that day. I used curse words heavily back then, and I remember not feeling right about it anymore. I had a new personality. I had become bold and carefree! That same year, I was baptized and made a public declaration of my faith in Jesus Christ.

> Behold, I will do a new thing; now it shall spring forth; shall ye not know it? I will even make a way in the wilderness, and rivers in the desert. (Isaiah 43:19)

The Crossroad

One Sunday, a guest speaker preached at our church. During the altar call, she prophesied to my mother and me and revealed the secret of our relationship. The evangelist stated these pivotal words in our hearts, "Jimmie, this is your daughter, and baby, this is your mother. She may not have birthed you into this world, but she is going to birth you in the Spirit." I didn't understand what she meant by that, but I knew it was a good thing.

Equipped with the Holy Ghost of God, a fiery church family, and a loving mother, I was ready to take on the kingdom of darkness, or so I thought. I had one problem, my past. Initially, my ministry started strong because I was zealous and confident. The only thing I talked about was the new birth experience. I preached at school, at home, at church, and at the adoptive agency as an alumnus to other foster kids. The agency would use my mother and me as a standard to follow during sensitive transitions. Our story inspired those already in placement as well as those just beginning.

If you asked me about the devil back then, I would have told you he was the witches and warlocks on television. I would have said he was the magic on Disney. I was still spiritually blind and immature. The Word of God says,

> No weapon that is formed against thee shall pros-
> per; and every tongue that shall rise against thee
> in judgment thou shalt condemn. (Isaiah 43:19)

The thing was, the weapons were being formed, and at the time, I was taking the hits and had no clue that the enemy could use the people who were closest to me. I saw people, not spirits. I took them at their word and did not understand spiritual warfare. I thought I was invincible. I had so much coverage I had forgotten about covering myself. I leaned hard on the special people in my life that I did not bother to fortify my faith and become an independent soldier. I grew lazy and did things inadequately. The devil attacked me through temptation, accusation, and guilt. I was easily led astray, like giving candy to a baby. Satan used many distractions to lure me away from the Word of God. I do not blame anyone because, ultimately, it was my decision to follow him, but I must expose the strategy of Satan to the one who may be unfamiliar with his evil ways as I was.

Remember I had a past, and I dealt heavily with the spirit of rejection. I needed deliverance as well from the sexual spirit that had entered in through the abuse I went through. There was so much I needed to learn but did not express because I cared more about finding my biological mom. I could not recognize the signs. And if I am speaking honestly, my foster mother tried, but I turned her down. For example, I was thirteen or fourteen when she asked me if I wanted to be adopted, but I told her no. What I was really telling her was "No, do not take me from my biological family because I am not ready to be steadfast."

> And Ruth said, Intreat me not to leave thee, or to return from following after thee: for whither thou goest, I will go; and where thou lodgest, I will lodge: thy people shall be my people, and thy God my God. (Ruth 1:16)

Every now and again, my foster mother would look at me and very directly say these words in a bitter tone, "I see you wanna learn the hard way, huh?" Both of my sisters were worldly, but I was in a home that was watering me with Scripture and Christlike character. They disagreed with my lifestyle and felt like my mama was turning me into an old fart. They felt like she was robbing me of my childhood, and I needed to be more like them. Bloomfield was a small town, and word carried around like quicksand.

Just about everyone in school knew that we were all sisters because we resembled one another, and we lived in proximity. My sisters were already in Bloomfield before I got back to the town, so they were planted. We were excited to hang out again although it was short-lived. My oldest sister moved out of town and finished high school somewhere else, but she kept in touch. My mother, being the evangelist that she was, allowed my oldest sister to stay with us every so often on the weekends. She opened her home, and because my sister was much older than me, she allowed her to babysit while she went to work. My sister and I could paint the town together, except she liked boys. I soon figured out I was not her first choice for coming back into town. One day, I mustered up enough courage to tell her that I saw she was only at my house to see her boyfriends. She would pacify me and tell me that we would do something fun after we went on her afternoon rendezvous. I chose not to discern the sign that we were being raised differently.

My other sister was a year older than me, and as she got older, she made her presence known. She was a fighter just like the oldest, except she fought a tad bit differently. I had enemies and bullies, and this one spoke up for me. And a fight came along with it if I had a problem. She was protective at all costs. I don't feel so special because she did this even for the underdog. This was the kind of person she was. She had a bold spirit in her, and I looked up to her because of it. She and our oldest sister were in one accord, but our oldest sister did not do a lot of talking. I respected my sisters because I saw their gifts and longed to be like them.

I had the biggest mouth of the three of us, except now it was being put to good use. My preaching was heard all around town, until one day, something struck the physical realm that I could not foresee. My sister, the fighter, was standing at the school bus stop, which was one stop early from mine. I got off to give her a hug and catch up for a bit before going our separate ways. As soon as I approached her, she slapped me across the face and told me I was an embarrassment to her. She demanded that I stop preaching about Jesus. I told her that I wasn't, that people were coming to me and asking me questions, and I answered them. She said that I represented her, not my foster family and not Jesus.

I was at the end of my eighth-grade year when that incident occurred. She yelled at me, threatening me not to bring that to the high school or else. When I got to high school, I would see her sometimes. We were not in the same grade, but she would come find me and surprise me. There were several events that I attended where she would be there to support me but, at the same time, judge my appearance. For example, my sister would hike up my skirt and unbutton the top part of my shirt because she felt like I was dressing too old for my age. She would also say that I was too pretty for makeup. At my chorus concert, she pulled me into the bathroom and showed me my face. She said, "Look at how beautiful you are." She did her best to get me to look at my flesh instead of my spirit. I would try to teach her about what my mother taught me about beauty and boys, but that angered her even more. She thought I was upstaging her.

> Yea, and all who will live a godly life in Christ
> Jesus shall suffer persecution. (2 Timothy 3:12)

Both my sisters thought my mother was turning me into an old frump and that it did not take all that to serve God. I became curious and interested in what they were trying to tell me around the age of nineteen. I thought I was missing out on something. I cared about my relationships with my sisters, and I did not want to lose them. In '97, my oldest sister invited all her siblings to her high school graduation and surprised us. I was sitting with my brother on one side of the auditorium, and two of my sisters were on the other side. My oldest sister was up singing a song for her class, and then we heard a loud voice shout from behind. As I turned around, I saw a woman staring directly at me with water-filled eyes. I knew immediately who it was. As we embraced, we walked to the front foyer where we all took turns hugging our mother and crying inconsolably. She could not stop saying sorry over and over in my ear, so I took the moment to do what the evangelist taught me. I told her that she was forgiven.

Apparently, my oldest sister had an agenda, and that was to keep our family together the best way she knew how. She did not understand the severity of what she was doing. She honestly believed she was doing the right thing, but that evening taught me a huge lesson. When I got home, I told my evangelist mother, what occurred, and she gave me a much-needed perspective. She took every occasion to apply Scripture to the challenges I faced. My mother said that my sister was having a hard time moving forward and that if I am not careful, I would end up just like her, stuck in the past. I became double-minded and played both sides of the fence concerning my families. To please my foster mother, I followed through on her rules, and to please my biological family, I came into agreement with their ways. Essentially, I was a people pleaser.

> And Saul said unto Samuel, "I have sinned; for I have transgressed the commandment of the Lord and thy words, because I feared the people and obeyed their voice." (1 Samuel 15:24)

> He who loves father or mother more than Me is not worthy of Me. And he who loves son or daughter more than Me is not worthy of Me. (Matthew 10:37)

> But let him ask in faith, nothing wavering. For he that waver is like a wave of the sea driven with the wind and tossed. For let not that man think that he shall receive any thing of the Lord. A double minded man is unstable in all his ways. (James 1:6–8)

My oldest sister had no choice but to fall back from me because my mother protected me from her ambition once she saw her error. My other sister moved out of her home, and the town altogether, for her own reasons. With fewer distractions, my mother was able to continue her job in raising me. I moved on with my life and did well for the most part with fewer distractions. I started working the year I turned fifteen. This was the same year I got hit with yet another distraction from my walk with Jesus Christ. A young man in the community desired to date me, and I was interested in boys at this point. I told him yes. My mother disapproved of my interest in boys. She said that I needed to focus on school and wait on the Lord and marriage for a coed relationship.

> But they that wait upon the Lord shall renew
> their strength; they shall mount up with wings as
> eagles; they shall run, and not be weary; and they
> shall walk, and not faint. (Isaiah 40:31)

One evening, my mother picked up the landline to listen to him and me talk. She overheard him say he loved me, and I said it in return. As I hung up feeling all gooey inside, I turned around, and there my mother stood. She questioned my love for him by asking if I meant it. I could not lie to my mother; my mother had eyes that peered through my soul anyway. She would tell me that it was the power of discernment. I told her I did not want to leave him hanging, so I said it too.

My mother was always honest no matter how it came across. She would say, "I am not here to be your friend. I am here to do my job, and that is to teach you the right way." Then she said, "Stop lying to that boy and stop lying to yourself." I ended up dating him all four years of high school. I wasn't with him to love him; I was dating him for security. He was dating me for the same reason, except his security came in the form of sex, and mine came in the form of attention. When he found out I would not perform such a dishonor, he dumped me and dated a freshman who did. I later found out he dumped her and then returned to me after he got what he wanted.

The relationship with him took my heart from the relationship I had with the Lord. I did not discern I was in yet another distraction. After a while, my preaching became compromised. I did not feel like preaching anymore because I had a new love now.

One day at work, a young man about age twenty-four walked in with his friend and made a purchase. I remember being loud and thirsty for attention. My coworker took his order while I was talking and playing toward the back. He stopped me when I walked to the front and handed me his pager number and said these words to me, "How old are you?"

I told him, "Nineteen."

He said, "I like the way you talk. You sound mature for your age."

Then he handed me his pager number and requested that I call him in a few years. In a matter of seconds, I forgot I had a four-year-old relationship with a young man at school.

> Stand fast therefore in the liberty wherewith
> Christ hath made us free and be not entangled
> again with the yoke of bondage. (Galatians 5:1)

Once known as the Jesus girl, church girl, Holy Roller, and many other creative names the students came up with, all that changed drastically. I used my money to purchase clothing that fit tight and made me look thirsty. All the teachers who once complimented me started advising me that I was changing but not for good. They held their heads down in shame. I started dating that young man, and he was poisonous. His heart was filled with bitterness because he had not forgiven people who had hurt him. He was unlearned in the Scriptures. He started giving me his worldly wisdom, and the Word that I learned at home began to escape my mind. I found out that I was not in the relationship for his words but for security.

Backslidden

Overall, my school experience did improve academically and socially. I graduated with my class, and it felt great. I remember being glad that I listened to my mother and stayed the course. I was still struggling to decide what I was going to do with my future, although I had become burned out with school, the system, and the journey! After graduation in 2003, I entered a community college but quit after I realized that I had to take some courses before starting college courses. I was discouraged and impatient. I began to follow the road of passion rather than patience. I perused the streets looking for something to do that fed my flesh-eating appetite. After a couple of dates and missed curfews, my mother raised her head, her eyes looking over her glasses at me walking through the door.

She said, "Now, Shelly, are you tired of doing right?" My mother tried to rescue me many times before. She did that to see her child walk the stage, but I was of age at this point.

There was an evening when I got back home from a date with the man, and she came outside to give him a biblical word of exhortation. I was embarrassed instead of realizing what a protective mother she was. I had become self-absorbed and conceited. I wasn't using the wisdom that I had been taught, so it was slipping away.

> For unto everyone that hath shall be given, and he shall have abundance; but from him that hath not, shall be taken away even that which he hath. (Matthew 25:29)

> Pride goeth before destruction, and an haughty spirit before a fall. (Proverbs 16:18)

One evening after another missed curfew, my mother had a hard talk with me. She did not fuss at me, and she did not bat an eye. She told me that I could not live in her house and disobey the rules. I made the decision to leave, and these were her words to me. She warned me, saying, "Don't start running like how your mother did, and don't get a reprobate mind."

I felt the warning chill my soul, and with those final words, I was gone. My older sister had an apartment by this time and had already told me that if I ever needed a place to stay, I could live with her, and that was the next door I walked through. I felt like trash leaving my mother that way, but I could not meet her expectations. I wanted to play and have fun. She wanted me to believe and work to build my dreams. I went to my sister's house thinking that was where I belonged. It also felt like I fit in. She and my oldest sister had jobs and their own places. They were in relationships and had one child each.

As soon as I got to my sister's house, I met a young man and lost my virginity within months of being there. My sister did not want me to date him because he was in a relationship with a lady up the street and had her pregnant. I did not listen because I thought I was better than anything else he was doing, coupled with the fact that he told me what he had going on would not stand in the way. What happened after that changed my life forever!

He began to show sorrow, depression, and oppression because the woman, who was twelve years his senior, had committed adultery, and her husband wanted him dead for what they had done. She was his braider, and one thing led to another. His situation was deeper than I could ever imagine, and what was worse was I was chasing after his heart, and he was chasing after her heart. What a vicious whirlwind. I pitied him, but it did not stop me from seeking after my needs. God intervened on my behalf to get me out of that tornado. I lived from pillar to post for almost nine months running behind this dead relationship, and my oldest sister was the one whom God used.

She was dropping me off at an apartment I obtained with him, and I went there looking for him. As I stepped out of her car, she said, "Shell, get out while you can. Think about it. You don't have any babies, and if you did, then you would be stuck with him and the situation."

Her words brought clarity. I got rid of the pride within and cried my sorry out in my mother's lap as I begged to go back home.

> For if any be a hearer of the word, and not a doer,
> he is like unto a man beholding his natural face
> in a glass: For he beholdeth himself, and goeth his
> way, and straightway forgetteth what manner of
> man he was. (James 1:23–24)

> When I was a child, I spake as a child, I under-
> stood as a child, I thought as a child: but when
> I became a man, I put away childish things. (1
> Corinthians 13:11–13)

Going back home was short-lived. My mother was engaged to be married. She taught me that if you wait on the Lord, then he will bless you in your season. I heard the word "wait," and that bothered me. I did not want to wait on anything. I was led by my emotions, and passion drove me around the city, trying to find security. I was happy for my mom, but I kept thinking that her wisdom only applied to her life, not mine.

> But seek ye first the kingdom of God, and his
> righteousness; and all these things shall be added
> unto you. (Matthew 6:33)

I left my new roots to return to my dead roots. I ended up on the run, just like my biological mom did at thirteen. Leaving home was a greater cost, and I was oblivious to the portion the Lord had given me through the new foundation that was built through my foster family on my behalf. Running, I began to walk in the same pattern as she. She was insecure and looking for love in all the wrong places. She sought out a fairy-tale romance that did not exist. She had her first child at nineteen, and I had mine at twenty. She started a family at twenty-one years old, and I started mine at twenty-two. Unbeknownst to me, I was imitating the dead journey of an insecure woman. It wasn't until a decade later that I truly came to realize the monumental generational cycle that needed to be destroyed!

To be continued…